Chameleon's CAN of WORMS

PICTURE BOOK APOLOGETICS *with* JAMES & RUTH

by J.D. CAMORLINGA

Picture Book Apologetics, Whittier 2013

Printed in the United States of America

First Printing, 2013

All scripture quotations, unless otherwise indicated, are taken from the Holy Bible, New International Version®, NIV®. Copyright ©1973, 1978, 1984, 2011 by Biblica, Inc.™ Used by permission of Zondervan. All rights reserved worldwide. www.zondervan.com The "NIV" and "New International Version" are trademarks registered in the United States Patent and Trademark Office by Biblica, Inc.™

ISBN 978-0615925356

Picture Book Apologetics
Whittier, CA

www.PictureBookApologetics.com

ACKNOWLEDGEMENTS

We give all glory to the Father who created us, to the Son who redeemed us and to the Spirit who sealed us; Praise be to Him!

DEDICATION

For the children of Grace Evangelical Free Church, and for inquisitive young minds everywhere; you are the future champions of the faith. May you grow in the wisdom of God, confident that what you believe is true!

James and Ruth love to fish in the creek.

Early in the morning, they run to the creek with rods and bait, find a quiet spot to cast their lines, and wait.

One day, while they were fishing and watching the fish swim here and there, James looked down at his can of worms; it was empty!

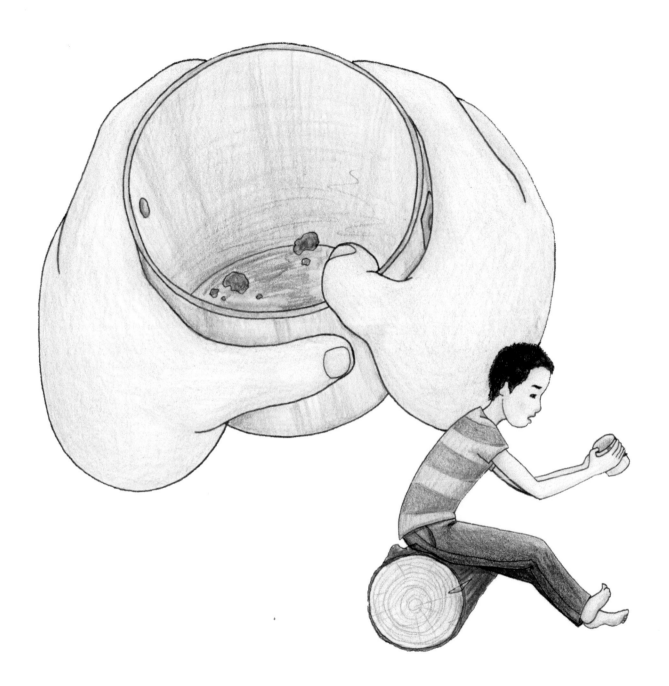

"Oh no," James groaned. "My bait is all gone!
I must have lost count of my worms."

"You can use some of mine," Ruth offered, but as she reached into her can of bait, she found that all of her worms were gone, too!

"What in the world?" she gasped. "Not a single worm left? I'm sure I didn't use them all!"

Just then, they noticed a chameleon lounging on the rock beside them.
She looked at them with one big, boogly eye and patted her belly.

"Thanks for the worms!" she laughed.

"Hey, Chameleon," James exclaimed, "that was our fishing bait! If you had asked we would have gladly shared, but it was wrong for you to steal like that."

"Says who?" Chameleon asked defiantly, fixing one boogly eye on James and one boogly eye on Ruth.

"The Bible teaches us that we should not steal. No one likes to have things stolen from them! It is wrong to steal," James replied, but Chameleon just laughed again and shook her head.

"It is wrong for **you** to tell **me** what I should or shouldn't do," Chameleon said. "Just because you think something is wrong, doesn't mean I have to think so, too. Don't tell me what to do!"

Now, James and Ruth's mom was working in the garden nearby and overheard all that Chameleon said. She walked down to the creek and gave James and Ruth a new can of worms from the garden.

"The Bible does tell us that some things are wrong to do," Mom said. "I'd like to ask you a question, Chameleon. **You** just told them something is wrong, so why is it bad for **them** to do the same?"

Chameleon rolled both of her big, boogly eyes, "Well, maybe what is wrong for you isn't wrong for me. The Bible may be true for you, but it isn't true for me."

"It sounds to me like you want us to believe we can't know if something is true for everyone. You want to pick and choose what is true. Is that correct?" Mom asked.

"That's right," Chameleon agreed. "Nothing is true for everyone all of the time!"

"Kids," Mom said, "Chameleon is talking about something called relative truth. Now, that doesn't mean 'relative' like Grandma or Uncle. It means something is only true sometimes and only for people who agree it is true."

"James, let's pretend there is a great big shark swimming by. What if **I** think it is a goldfish? Does that make it a goldfish?"

James stifled a giggle. "Mom, you're being silly! It's a shark!"

"You're right, James!" Mom said. "Even if I don't believe it is a shark, it is still true that it is a shark. That is why our family believes there is something called absolute truth. Do you know what 'absolute truth' means?"

Ruth thought for a moment. "Does it mean that something is always true even if people don't agree it is true?"

"That is exactly right! Good job, Ruth," Mom said.

"But," Chameleon sputtered. "You can't
know for *sure* that something is true!"

Mom answered gently. "You are saying that you *know for sure* that you *can't* know anything for sure! That is like **saying** 'I can't talk!' Do you understand why that doesn't make sense?"

Chameleon slowly nodded her head. Her eyes wobbled here and there. She had a lot to think about.

Ruth and James took turns forgiving Chameleon for stealing their worms.

Mom beamed. "I'm proud of you two. I'm glad you understand that something can be true even if people disagree. Words like 'relative' and 'absolute' can be hard to think about, but it is important to know why you believe what you believe and if what you believe is true. May I sit with you while you fish?"

"Of course, Mom!" James exclaimed. "Fish with us, Chameleon!"

Then James, Ruth, Mom and Chameleon sat together by the creek, watching the fish swim here and there, and enjoying each other's company; and that is the truth.

Practical Exercise

Bring a favorite family treat to the table and divide evenly between you and your child(ren). Then, before you eat the treat, take most of their share and add it to yours:

- How would your child feel about someone eating their share of the treat?
- Is taking something that belongs to someone else the right thing to do?
- Where do our moral values come from? (You may want to discuss the Ten Commandments and God's goodness)
- How do we live consistently with our values?
- Explain to your children that goodness and badness do not depend on personal opinion. Morals come from God.
- Redistribute the treat and enjoy together!
- "All your words are true; all your righteous laws are eternal." – Psalm 119:160

Find suggested reading and more resources written by experts in their fields, at
www.YouthApologeticsNetwork.com

Adults,

Moral relativism is a pervasive issue that we face today. Its brand of tolerance has seeped into popular literature, film, music and television programs. "What's true for you is not true for me" and "all religions are just different roads to God" are two familiar examples.

It is important that our children understand that truth is real and objective. It is important that they can identify truth, live by truth, and share truth with their friends.

Our hope is that this book will help you guide your child through a simple refutation of just such a "true for you but not for me" argument, while also equipping them to respond with courage and kindness when their beliefs are challenged. We pray that this book will inspire deep conversations between you and your children about our matchless Creator, and will encourage them to love Him in ever-deepening ways.

In Christ,
J.D. Camorlinga

RELATIVISM IN ACTION

"You have your way, I have my way. As for the right way, it does not exist."
– Friedrich Nietzsche

"There is nothing either good or bad, but thinking makes it so." – *Hamlet*

Without absolute truth it is impossible to condemn immoral actions. A person who believes morals are relative would be unable to judge whether murdering the innocent or stealing from the poor are evil acts.

RELATIVISM IS SELF-REFUTING

1) "There are no universal, objective truths about the world." We'll call that premise 1.

2) The relativist holds that premise 1 is an abstract (or metaphysical) claim about the world. In other words, they believe premise 1 is true.

3) If premise 1 is true, then premise 1 is a universal, objective truth.

4) Premise 3 contradicts premise 1. This is a logical fallacy known as Contradictory Premises (a.k.a. logical paradox).

5) Therefore, relativism is false.

Also available from Picture Book Apologetics:

Pig and the Accidental Oink
(The Kalām cosmological argument)

Chameleon's Can of Worms
(Defense against relativism)

Coming Soon:

Proving Christianity with the resurrection

Made in the USA
Middletown, DE
03 April 2022